COVENANT • BIBLE • STUDIES

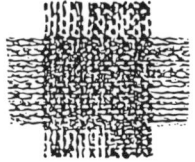

Hymns and Songs of the Bible

Mary Anne Parrott

```
220.07 P249h c.2
Parrott, Mary Anne, 1943-
Hymns and songs of the Bible
```

faithQuest® ♦ Brethren Press®

Covenant Bible Studies Series

Copyright © 1998 by *faithQuest*®. Published by Brethren Press®, 1451 Dundee Avenue, Elgin, IL 60120.

All rights reserved. No portion of this book may be reproduced in any form or by any process or technique without the written consent of the publisher, except for brief quotations embodied in critical articles or reviews.

Unless otherwise noted, scripture quotations are from the New Revised Standard Version of the Bible, copyrighted 1989 by the National Council of Churches of Christ in the USA, Division of Education and Ministry.

Cover photo: David B. Van Delinder

02 01 00 99 98   5 4 3 2 1

Library of Congress Cataloging-in-Publication Data
Parrott, Mary Anne, 1943-
   Hymns and songs of the Bible/Mary Anne Parrott.
      p.   cm. --(Covenant Bible studies)
   Includes bibliographical references.
   ISBN 0-87178-014-3 (alk. paper)
      1. Hymns in the Bible--Study and teaching.
      2. Bible--Prayers--Study and teaching.
         I. Title.   II. Series: Covenant Bible study series.
BS680.H94P37 1998
220'.071--DC21   98-22517

Manufactured in the United States of America

Contents

Foreword vii
Preface ix
1. Sing Aloud to God Our Strength 1
2. Sing to the Lord in the Company of the Faithful:
   Hymns of Praise 6
3. You Set the Earth on Its Foundation:
   Creation Hymns 11
4. Restore Us Again!: Songs of Lament 15
5. Songs of Thanksgiving 20
6. Here Is My Servant, My Chosen:
   Servant Songs 24
7. My Soul Magnifies the Lord: Nativity Songs 28
8. The Greatest of These: Hymns of Love 33
9. The Image of the Invisible God: Hymns of Faith.... 37
10. Worthy Is the Lamb: Hymns in Revelation 41
Suggestions for Sharing and Prayer 46

Foreword

The Covenant Bible Studies Series was first developed for a denominational program in the Church of the Brethren and the Christian Church (Disciples of Christ). This program, called People of the Covenant, was founded on the concept of relational Bible study and has been adopted by several other denominations and small groups who want to study the Bible in a community rather than alone.

Relational Bible study is marked by certain characteristics, some of which differ from other types of Bible study. For one, it is intended for small groups of people who can meet face-to-face on a regular basis and share frankly with an intimate group. It is important to remember that relational Bible study is anchored in covenantal history. God covenanted with people in Old Testament history, established a new covenant in Jesus Christ, and covenants with the church today.

Relational Bible study takes seriously a corporate faith. As each person contributes to study, prayer, and work, the group becomes the real body of Christ. Each one's contribution is needed and important. "For just as the body is one and has many members, and all the members of the body, though many, are one body, so it is with Christ. . . . Now you are the body of Christ and individually members of it" (1 Cor. 12:12,17).

Relational Bible study helps both individuals and the group to claim the promise of the Spirit and the working of the Spirit. As one person testified, "In our commitment to one another and in our sharing, something happened. . . . We were woven together in love by the Master Weaver. It is something that can happen only when two or three or seven are gathered in God's name, and we know the promise of God's presence in our lives."

For people who choose to use this study in a small group, the following guidelines will help create an atmosphere in which support will grow and faith will deepen.

1. As a small group of learners, we gather around God's word to discern its meaning for today.
2. The words, stories, and admonitions we find in scripture come alive for today, challenging and renewing us.
3. All people are learners and all are leaders.

4. Each person will contribute to the study, sharing the meaning found in the scripture and helping to bring meaning to others.
5. We recognize each other's vulnerability as we share out of our own experience, and in sharing we learn to trust others and to be trustworthy.

Additional suggestions for study and group-building are provided in the "Sharing and Prayer" section. They are intended for use in the hour preceding the Bible study to foster intimacy in the covenant group and relate personal sharing to the Bible study topic.

Welcome to this study. As you search the scriptures, may you also search yourself. May God's voice and guidance and the love and encouragement of brothers and sisters in Christ challenge you to live more fully the abundant life God promises.

Preface

The first thing that comes to my mind when I think of Bible songs are those little scripture ditties we learned as children in Sunday school: "Zacchaeus was a wee little man," "So rise and shine, and give God the glory, glory," "Beloved, let us love one another." You and your covenant group can probably think of dozens more. They stick with us in an era that has largely dispensed with memory work and provide finger holds on scripture that might otherwise have disappeared from our consciousness.

This study explores Bible songs, but not the two-line gems from childhood rug-sitting sessions. These are the songs and poetry of the Bible: psalms of praise, creation hymns, laments, songs of thanksgiving, Isaiah's Servant Songs, the songs heralding Jesus' nativity, Christ hymns, and the majestic hymns of Revelation. The major focus will be on texts and how they were part of the life and worship of the faith community.

We will also connect the themes of the biblical songs with Christian hymnody, so keep your hymnals handy. As you read through the study, note the many references to *Hymnal: A Worship Book* (HWB) and the *Chalice Hymnal* (CH). If at all possible, secure a copy of one of these two hymnals for each participant. Otherwise, another denominational hymnal will be an important supplement to your study.

Thousands of years of hymnwriting have left us a musical legacy as theologically rich as the Bible itself. But it is the music, combined with the texts, that can transport us to a different space, that can evoke in us emotion and desire and strength that is attributable to the mysterious activity of God's Spirit. No one can promise when it will happen, but we must sing or play to go there . . .

Here are some suggestions for enhancing this study of the music of the Bible and later hymnody.

1. Write a hymn. The following suggestions may assist you if you are inexperienced: (a) Pick a theme, such as praising God the Creator. (b) Pick a familiar melody. A regular, frequently used meter is a good beginning. Check your hymnal's metrical index. (c) Outline each verse. For example, in a hymn praising God as

Creator, you might plan three verses around the three themes: attributes of God as Creator; creation of the universe and our world; creation of humanity—our role as co-creators with God of community, love, justice. Then expand the third verse with a call to respond in lives of thankful praise.

2. Between covenant meetings memorize a hymn. Soon you'll have made several new hymns your own. Sing these hymns to yourself from time to time, and use them as you pray.
3. If you have books available on the sources of hymns (check with your pastor or try the library in your community), look up some of your favorite hymns. Think of ways to share this information, such as writing a series of articles in your church newsletter.
4. If you know someone who can teach you American Sign Language, learn the signs of a few key words. Or a book such as *The Joy of Signing* by Lottie L. Riekehof (Gospel Publishing House, Springfield, Mo., 1987) has a good selection of signs used in Christian contexts. For instance, the sign for "holy" is the word for "clean" made with the H hand position. Incorporate movement into your singing, perhaps in a responsive, lining-out fashion (leader sings and signs a line, congregation repeats it, etc.).
5. Keep a notebook. It could include several sections: (a) List all hymns (or other music based on hymns—prelude, anthem, etc.) used in your church. Analyze how they relate to the biblical categories of hymns we are studying (as listed above and in the table of contents). Note any direct allusions to stories or texts in the Bible. (b) List all songs in the Bible that you discover. Find ways to incorporate them into meditation and prayer. (c) Include your own creations—songs, poems, prayers, journaling, visual art.

Resources for This Study

The *Chalice Hymnal* (Chalice Press, Disciples of Christ denominational hymnal) contains an abbreviated Psalter, complete with instructions for using the psalms responsively.

Hymnal: A Worship Book (Brethren Press, Faith & Life Press, Mennonite Publishing House) is the denominational hymnal of churches in the Believers Church tradition.

Hymnal Companion (Brethren Press, Faith & Life Press, Mennonite Publishing House) provides detailed histories about the people and circumstances that produced the hymns and resources found in *Hymnal: A Worship Book*.

Preface

The *Psalter Hymnal* (CRC Publications, Christian Reformed Church denominational hymnal) contains at least one musical setting of each psalm.

For Additional Reading

"Introduction to the Psalms," *The New Oxford Annotated Bible* (NRSV). Oxford University Press, 1991.

Baird, William. *I Corinthians, II Corinthians* (Knox Preaching Guides). John H. Hayes, ed. John Knox Press, 1980.

Berrigan, Daniel. *Isaiah—Spirit of Courage, Gift of Tears*. Augsburg Fortress, 1996.

Brueggemann, Walter. *The Message of the Psalms: A Theological Commentary*. Augsburg Publishing House, 1984.

Brueggemann, Walter. *The Psalms and the Life of Faith*. Patrick D. Miller, ed. Augsburg Fortress, 1995.

Craddock, Fred B. *Luke* (Interpretation Series). John Knox Press, 1990.

Dunn, James D. G. *Commentary on Colossians and Philemon*. William B. Eerdmans, 1996.

Fiorenza, Elisabeth Schussler. *Revelation: Vision of a Just World* (Proclamation Commentaries Series). Gerhard Krodel, ed. Fortress Press, 1992.

Stuhlmueller, Carroll, C.P. *Psalms 1 and 2*. Michael Glazier, Inc., 1983.

Whybray, R.N. *The New Century Bible Commentary, Isaiah 40–66*. Wm. B. Eerdmans, 1975.

1

Sing Aloud to God Our Strength
Psalm 100; Psalm 81:1-5a; Ephesians 5:15-20

> *All people that on earth do dwell,*
> *sing out your faith with cheerful voice;*
> *delight in God whose praise you tell,*
> *whose presence calls you to rejoice.*
>
> —William Kethe, 1561 (HWB 42, CH 18)

Personal Preparation

1. Think of a hymn or stanza that expresses your faith. Recall situations or people you associate with the hymn. Use it daily this week in meditation and prayer.
2. If you were in a crisis, what hymn do you think would come to your lips? Why? (This hymn may or may not be the same one you listed above.)
3. Read Psalm 100 and Psalm 81. Try to imagine what kind of music *you* think would go with it. What kind of tune would bring out the character and tone of the words?
4. Now read Psalm 100 and the hymn "All People That on Earth Do Dwell" (HWB 42, CH 18). In his rendition of Psalm 100, has Kethe brought out any nuances that help you hear the psalm in a new way?

Understanding

Old Testament. As an organist, I have played for several dozen weddings in a variety of churches. Very early in this career it became evident to me that one piece of music, "Jubal's Lyre," was the ideal music to play after the recessional—something dignified, yet lively. I played it for many years before I knew it was named for one of three men listed in the seventh generation of the Genesis genealogy: Jubal, "the ancestor of all those who play the lyre and pipe" (Gen. 4:21).

As Israel remembered, reflected on, and recorded its history, music energized their memories and worship. In the time of King David, worship gradually formalized as David ordered the ark of the covenant, that mobile sanctuary of God, to be moved to a more permanent place in Jerusalem. When the ark ceased moving, worship also settled in. The four thousand Levites David chose to lead temple worship (see 1 Chron. 15:16-24) put existing tunes—shepherd tunes of four to six notes—with new sacred texts. These new texts were "psalms" ("praises" in Hebrew). The Book of Psalms, also called the psalter, was the hymnal of ancient Israel, compiled from older collections of lyrics for use in the temple. A "hymn" is one type of psalm and refers to acts of praise suitable for worship in the temple.

The psalms that "made it" into the psalter were carefully crafted. Notice the parallel phrases in Psalm 100 below: the second phrase completes the thought of the first or rewords it. It is as if the writer is saying, "A, and what's more, B." This is *parallelism*, a central feature of Hebrew poetry, which forms about one-third of the Old Testament.

Psalm 100

(*Phrase*)
Make a joyful noise to the Lord,
    all the earth.
(*Parallel*)
Worship the Lord with gladness;
    come into his presence with singing.

(*Phrase*)
Know that the Lord is God.
    It is he that made us,
    and we are his;
(*Parallel*)
    we are his people,
    and the sheep of his pasture.

(*Phrase*)
Enter his gates with thanksgiving,
    and his courts with praise.
(*Parallel*)
Give thanks to him, bless his name.

Sing Aloud to God Our Strength

(*Phrase*)
For the Lord is good;
His steadfast love endures forever,
(*Parallel*)
and his faithfulness to all
generations.

A psalm for everyone. Like popular music, the Psalms tap the spectrum of human experience, emotions, and faith. They run the gamut from the image of God as a shepherd to an alphabet book, to a wedding ceremony, to traveling songs. Seeing that the people in biblical times were dealing with the same issues as contemporary artists will help bring those ancient writings to life. It's a comfort to realize we aren't the only ones who feel giddy joy, deep depression, hot anger, the perplexing pull between trust and mistrust, a gnawing sense of injustice, general confusion about why things are the way things are, and the longing to relax and become one with nature.

For instance, Psalm 100 speaks to us when our confidence in God is strong and the current of joy runs deep. It is a psalm of thanksgiving.

Psalm 81, on the other hand, is appropriate for covenant renewal. Imagine it as part of the liturgy of the Feast of Tabernacles, also known as the Feast of Booths—the clues are in verse 3 especially: "Blow the trumpet at the new moon, at the full moon, on our festal day." Trumpets heralded the celebration of the first day of the month (new moon) and again at the full moon (15th day). The latter half of the psalm reminds Israel of the desert wanderings, of God's urgent reaching to a people who sabotaged themselves by turning away from the divine hand that nurtured them. This search is, in fact, what the Feast of Booths is all about: an annual recounting of the flight from Egypt, of how "I made the people of Israel live in booths when I brought them out of the land of Egypt" (Lev. 23:43).

New Testament. The psalter was the first hymnbook of the early church as well as for Israel. But the Book of Psalms is not the only biblical source for poetry and hymn texts. In addition to the examples of hymns throughout the Old Testament (Song of Deborah in Judges 5, Canticle of Hannah in 1 Samuel 2:1-10, and Lamentations), hymns and hymn fragments are scattered throughout the New Testament, especially in Luke's birth stories (Magnificat in 1:47-55; Song of Zechariah in 1:67-79; Song of Simeon in 2:29-32), in the letters to the churches (the "Christ hymns" in Colossians 1:15-20 and in Philippians 2:5-11); in the doxologies that close the letters; and in the Book of Revelation (5:9-14; 15:3b-4; 19:1-8; 21:1-4).

Several references are made in the New Testament to "psalms and hymns and spiritual songs" (see Eph. 5:19; Col. 3:16). These terms are not clearly defined, but studied consensus points to the psalms as songs from the Hebrew Bible, hymns as new compositions with emphasis on Christ, and spiritual songs as more like folk songs with Christian language. The names "psalms" and "psalter" come from the Greek translation of the Old Testament (the Septuagint). Both words originally referred to stringed instruments (like harp, lute, lyre). Later, they also began to mean the songs those instruments accompanied.

In the New Testament there is no mention of musical instruments or church musicians. New Testament silence on these matters has led to controversies about their appropriateness in worship. But there are strong clues that congregational singing became a central part of early Christian worship. Singing was a part of the new life in Christ, especially linked to thanksgiving (Eph. 5:19; Col. 3:16), and it was the nature of the Christian community to be jubilant assemblies (Acts 2:46-47). We know that Paul encouraged the church at Corinth to write new songs for "building up" (1 Cor. 14:26).

A singing faith. We sing our faith. The twentieth-century mystic Thomas Merton once said, "Those whose vocation in the church is prayer find that they live on the psalms, for the psalms enter into every department of their life." Faith has three dimensions—*belief, trust,* and *action*—and the church's song has played a key role in keeping these vital dimensions connected.

> **Belief:** Our hymns put our theology into concise, poetic words; they tell God's wonderful story in language and cadence that's easy to remember.
>
> **Trust:** Music touches us at a deeply emotional (and physiological) level. Why else do people with Alzheimer's disease remember the songs of their youth when they remember little else? Coma patients have been known to mumble hymns when they can respond in no other way.
>
> **Action:** Communal song is a mighty motivator to action. People in every social or political movement have their songs—from the Hebrews to the Protestant reformers to African American slaves—to proclaim their identity and vision, to band together, and to fire up their members to action toward the common goals.

As we sing our faith, the unique power of poetic rhythm and imagery combined with the body language of music make indelible impressions upon us. A hymn is a poetic form that functions on an emotive/affective level. As we learn styles of faith music unfamiliar to us, we can experience faith on new levels: for example, chorales, rap, praise songs, hymns from other cultures, rock, plainsong, contemporary melodies. Variety is key.

Good hymns endure because they elicit from us an experience of God that threads through generations. A metrical psalm based on Psalm 100 from the mid-sixteenth century, "All People That on Earth Do Dwell," continues to find its place in new hymnals. The writer of the hymn, William Kethe, was a Scottish clergyman who probably fled persecution under the Catholic "Bloody Mary" in the mid 1550s. He may even have remained in exile in Geneva to help reformer John Calvin with psalms for the English-language Geneva Bible (1560). This book followed hard on the heels of the 1551 *Genevan Psalter*, a hymnal based solely on texts from the Psalms. Metrical psalms were one form of early Protestant hymns; Calvin, unlike Martin Luther, believed that only words of scripture were appropriate in hymns. The first tune used with Kethe's text is still known as OLD HUNDREDTH, because it was a setting of Psalm 100.

Discussion and Action

1. Some may wish to comment on their thinking (from Personal Preparation) by completing this sentence aloud: "One of the hymns that best expresses my faith [or theology] is _____ because _____."
2. Look through your congregation's hymnal. What does the introduction or preface tell you about how the hymnal committee chose hymns and worship aids for the book? Look at the table of contents. Does the organization reveal priorities and theology? Examine the various indexes in the back. How can each of these be helpful?
3. Do you know any churches that do not have musical instruments? Are there any instruments that are inappropriate for worship? Why?
4. If you could take only two CDs or tapes on a trip, what would they be? Why?
5. Encourage each member to pick a hymn project from the list in "Overall Suggestions" in the Preface.

2

Sing to the Lord in the Company of the Faithful
Psalm 46; Psalm 96; Psalm 113

See, the streams of living waters springing from eternal love,
well supply thy sons and daughters, and all fear of want remove.
Who can faint while such a river ever flows, their thirst t'assuage—
grace, which like the Lord the giver, never fails from age to age?

—John Newton, 1979 (st. 2— HWB 619, CH 709)

Personal Preparation

1. Read Psalm 46. How is the psalm especially appropriate for public worship? private prayer? Look up any of the following hymns that contain allusions to it:
    "A Mighty Fortress Is Our God" (CH 65, HWB 165)
    "Shall We Gather at the River" (CH 701, HWB 615)
    "Glorious Things of Thee Are Spoken"
       (CH 709, HWB 619)
    "Sing Praise to God Who Reigns Above" (CH 6, HWB 59)
   How is God your "refuge and strength"?
2. Listen to a Christian rock radio station if there is one in your broadcast area. Ask one or more teenagers to loan you any pop Christian music CDs or tapes they have, and listen to them. Choose some with themes of praise to share with your covenant group.
3. Read Psalm 113. In your experience, does (or has) God raised the poor and needy from the dust (v. 7)? Do the poor find equality with the rich (v. 8)? Do couples unable to have children become parents (v. 9)? Is this a psalm of praise or a psalm of hope? Is there a difference?

Understanding

Praise is scarce. We live in a North American culture that dwells on *scarcity* even though we have garnered the riches of the world. Yet the faith of the Psalms is a trust in God's *abundance* expressed in "glad abandonment," to use a term of Old Testament and Psalms scholar Walter Brueggemann (*The Psalms and the Life of Faith*). The psalms of praise seek nothing but to celebrate with thankful joy. Have you ever felt a moment when you needed absolutely nothing except a way to say thank you?

Life is meant to be shared. "There is no life that is not lived in community and no community not lived in praise of God," wrote T. S. Eliot in "The Rock." In their ironic song about a rock, "I am a rock, I am an island," contemporary folk singers Simon and Garfunkel also sang about how hard it is to live in isolation.

Praise is essentially a communal phenomenon. Joy and thanksgiving, sorrow and risk are to be shared. Some of the most thrilling moments my spirit has ever known have occurred when I was singing with a choir or congregation—beautiful music and meaningful text sung with faithful, enthusiastic singers around me. Think of music you've experienced on holidays. How did you feel singing "Joy to the World" from memory and in harmony in a big group? That's communal praise.

The three psalms of praise upon which we focus here (46, 96, 113) are often referred to as "hymns" because they are public (community as opposed to intimate or personal) songs of praise to God for the nature of God's being or of God's creating and liberating actions.

A Zion hymn. Psalm 46 is a hymn of confidence; it begins with the familiar words "God is our refuge and strength, a very present help in trouble." It is associated with the invasion of the Assyrian king Sennacherib (701 B.C.), who laid waste to all of Judah, save Jerusalem, and then "miraculously" withdrew. Before Jerusalem fell in 587 B.C., the city had become the symbol of Israel's preservation. The psalm itself celebrates God's creation providing a refuge from natural chaos and the chaos of war. This psalm was the inspiration for Martin Luther's hymn "A Mighty Fortress Is Our God," in which Luther interprets God as a place of refuge. Fred Craddock also tells the story of asking a rabbi what his favorite imaging name for God was, since Jews do not call God directly by name. The rabbi's response: "The Place." Likewise, in Psalm 46 Jerusalem (Zion) symbolizes God's place and care.

Things are looking up. The theme of Psalm 96 is the majesty and awesomeness of God. This psalm, upon closer inspection, is a medley of other psalms and phrases from Isaiah 40–55. Like many "modern" hymns, it is a melding of existing poetic and theological thought into a new hymn form.

Walter Brueggemann, in *The Message of the Psalms*, identifies this as a psalm of "new orientation"—the psalm of a community that was "in the pit" (the Babylonian exile) and then receives an unexpected gift of grace and renewed stability. It is a summons to look up from despair and see the Divine.

A frame for worship. Psalm 113 begins and ends with a call to worship, and in between describes attributes of God to be praised, such as his power to save and to rule, his lifting up of the poor and needy. This psalm is traditionally sung at the great Jewish festivals, especially Passover. Jesus and his disciples likely sang it with Psalms 114–118 (the rest of the so-called "Egyptian Hallel") at the last supper, which was, of course, a paschal feast. The theme of Psalm 113 is God's intervention on behalf of the poor and needy. In *Weaving the New Creation*, James W. Fowler has described Psalm 113 as a "class action suit," which argues that God's main business is empowerment of "the least" in the community. To call Israel to worship, the psalmist also evokes the memory of the barren matriarchs such as Sarah and Hannah.

Who is this God who saves? Psalms of praise are extravagant in their descriptions of God and in their long list of God's saving actions. Old Testament hymns of praise typically begin with a call to praise, "O sing to the Lord a new song" (96:1), followed by reasons, "for great is the Lord . . . he is to be revered . . . [he] made the heavens . . . honor and majesty are before him . . . strength and beauty are in his sanctuary" (96:4-6). Notice that God is praised as a righteous judge (96:13), as One who cares for the poor and needy (113:7), as a refuge (46:1), as a world peacemaker (46:9). The community works together to create a list of the attributes of God, a stream-of-consciousness praising, one person's praise feeding off that of others, and vice versa.

The psalms of praise have inspired church music throughout the centuries, with many taking their texts directly from the psalms. Though the allusion to Psalm 46 is somewhat vague (st. 2 coincides with v. 4), the overall sense of John Newton's hymn "Glorious Things of Thee Are Spoken" is one of praise. Newton may well sing praise, because he experienced a dramatic conversion while he was a slave-ship captain in the second quarter of the 1700s. Newton was ordained later as a minister and was a prolific hymn writer. "Amazing Grace" is another of Newton's hymns that praises the grace of God.

A contemporary response. The past twenty-five-year period is remarkable for its explosion of creative new hymnody. The fallout is full of communal hymns of praise incorporating themes for the twentieth and twenty-first centuries, such as eco-justice and response to war, famine, and need. Check out hymns by Fred Pratt Green, Harry Emerson Fosdick, Kenneth Morse, Brian Wren, Ruth Duck, Thomas Troeger, and Christopher Idle that call believers to praise God through their loving response to need.

Like the syncopation of medieval tunes; the driving, foot-stomping, heartbeat rhythms of early American music (kept alive by Sacred Harp singers); the work-song lilt of African American spirituals, the chief characteristic of the various forms of today's pop music is rhythm. When the church wants to speak to contemporary problems facing our communities, it will find various ways to incorporate strong rhythm. How many of us have felt like swaying when singing "We Shall Overcome" (CH 630), or tapping to the rhythms of "In Your Sickness, Your Sufferings" (HWB 585), "Earth and All Stars" (HWB 47), or "For We Are Strangers No More" (HWB 322)?

And finally, whether or not we personally like the music, we can't ignore how contemporary praise music seems to draw people to worship. Though traditional and so-called "contemporary" worship often make for two congregations, can we strive to do both rather than either/or?

Praise may be "useless," but it is *essential*! It puts life in perspective; it forces us to look beyond ourselves. Participating in community and praising God are two of our most important connections with God. When a church meeting breaks apart in bickering and disagreement, it may not be easy to sing together, but praising God, singing, and building community are inextricably interwoven.

Discussion and Action

1. Read the last paragraph above. What are the implications of the claim that praise, singing, and community "are inextricably interwoven"? Is it possible to praise God *alone*? For how long?
2. Share the pop music CDs you discovered. Brainstorm ways some of this music might fit—if it doesn't already—into your congregation's worship life.

3. Sing as many hymns of praise as time allows. Choose at least one hymn with strong rhythm, and familiarize yourselves with songs from different eras that you can feel in your body as much as in your vocal chords. Tap out the rhythm on your chest as you sing, sway slightly with the beat, clap, shake keys, or drum on the table.
4. Attend together a worship service whose main theme is praise (e.g., Taizé, Pentecostal), or attend a contemporary Christian music concert. Debrief afterward.

3

You Set the Earth on Its Foundation: Creation Hymns
Psalm 104

*I sing the mighty pow'r of God, that made the mountains rise,
that spread the flowing seas abroad and built the lofty skies.
I sing the wisdom that ordained the sun to rule the day.
The moon shines full at God's command and all the stars obey.*

—Isaac Watts, 1715 (HWB 46)

Personal Preparation

1. Read Psalm 104. Look in your hymnal's indexes for hymns related to this psalm and the topic of creation. Sing some!
2. List all the verbs in Psalm 104 (or at least one from each verse). What does this collection of verbs tell you about the Creator? about creation?
3. List God's creations that hold special meaning for you. Choose one and elaborate on it in a story, poem, song, prayer, sketch, dance, or some other means of expression.
4. When you were a guest in a strange place, what made you feel welcome, comfortable, safe? What is done to help visitors/guests feel welcome and comfortable in your congregation? Does your congregation have a hospitality or welcoming committee or group? How does it work?

Understanding

In the Ancient Near East, hospitality was carefully choreographed. Hospitality was a necessity in a land where there were few Holiday Inns to be found along the interstate between the rivers Nile and Euphrates.

Hospitality was a religious mandate for the Jews, who hoped to be welcomed at God's own heavenly banquet. Being hospitable consisted particularly of protecting one's guest and providing the necessities of food, drink, and respite from the desert.

A lack of hospitality, not aberrant sexuality, was the sin of Sodom. The heinous intent of the "men of Sodom" was to do violence to strangers (who were revealed to be angels). Lot was the only one who treated the strangers as they ought to be treated: he took them in and protected them. Later, Ezekiel pronounced judgment on Sodom for being so wicked as to fail to aid the needy, in itself a woeful lack of hospitality (Ezek. 16:49).

On the other hand, Ancient Near East hospitality expected the stranger-become-guest not to overstay the welcome—three days, maximum. The *Midrash Tehillim* (rabbinical commentary on the scripture, in this case, the Psalms) says that a host is expected to slaughter a calf in his guest's honor on the first day, a sheep on the second, a fowl on the third. And the fourth day a host is not obligated to serve anything but beans. Also, any appreciative guest will sing the praises of the host.

From where does such a rigorous expectation of hospitality come? From no less than our Creator God, the ultimate host. Creation first reveals this to us. Notice the extravagance of imagery with which the writer of Psalm 104 describes God's provision: the earth planted on a firm foundation and the waters kept in their bounds; the necessities of life provided to humankind and the animals; and the ecology of life, which welcomes all creatures to their time and place. Indeed, the poet in Psalm 104 plays word games with Genesis 1, enhancing and embellishing it:

1st day—creation of light —Ps. 104:1-2a
2nd day—creation of firmament—Ps. 104:2b-4
3rd day—separation of heaven and earth—Ps. 104:5-9
4th day—sun, moon, stars—Ps. 104:19-20
5th day—fish created—Ps. 104:25-26
6th day—animals, humankind—Ps. 104:21-23, 27-28

The creator of Psalm 104 receives God's cosmic hospitality and generosity by singing the highest praises and promising to continue through life: "I will sing to the Lord as long as I live." But Israelites were not, of course, the only religious peoples in the Ancient Near East to recognize and sing the wonders of creation. According to Carroll Stuhlmueller, about a third of Psalm 104 is similar to Egyptian and Mesopotamian hymns, especially the Egyptian monotheist Akhenaten's hymn to the sun god Aten (1364–1376 B.C.) and hymns to the Mesopotamian god Enlil.

For Israel, creation was associated with the royalty of God, and it is likely that Psalm 104 was compiled for a kingly occasion, perhaps even the dedication of Solomon's temple. Both the psalm and the Genesis 1–2 accounts celebrate God's awesome creation and faithful hospitality.

So, too, we who are God's guests-become-friends will joyfully spread the good news. After all, as someone has said, "What is the Gospel if it is not one beggar telling another where to find food?" Some of my favorite hymns describe how all of creation praises God:

There's not a plant or flower below,
but makes your glories known . . .

—Isaac Watts, 1715 (HWB 46, CH 64)

All thy works with joy surround thee,
earth and heaven reflect thy rays . . .

—Henry van Dyke, 1907 (HWB 71, CH 2)

Read English composer Albert F. Bayly's creation poem "When the Morning Stars Together" (HWB 34). Bayly had already made lifestyle choices based on his interpretation of what it means to be hospitable in response to God's hospitality. He gave up his work as a shipbuilder when "work on warships ran contrary to his emerging pacifist views" and became, instead, a Congregational pastor in England (*Hymnal Companion*).

If you are able, get a copy of James Weldon Johnson's *God's Trombones* from your local library or church library. This contemporary rendition of the story of how God created a place for people—a hospitable place—was inspired by an African American preaching tradition that invites enthusiastic response. This collection of seven sermons in verse begins,

And God stepped out on space,
And he looked around and said:
I'm lonely—I'll make me a world.

After the first five days of creation, God sat down, still lonely: God thought and thought,

Till he thought: I'll make me a man! . . .
Then into it he blew the breath of life,
And man became a living soul. Amen. Amen.

This is also in the tradition of some creation psalms such as Psalm 8 in which humanity is both the climax and theme: ". . . what are human beings that you are mindful of them? . . . Yet you have made them a little lower than God."

Like a great sermon, like Johnson's poem, the hospitality of the created world demands an AMEN! response from us. Indeed, being created by God with such high esteem and love requires significant "response-ability." It requires the acceptance of God's hospitality.

The creation psalms extol how God's order provides stable, equitable, and generous living. But such equity and stability are achieved only where the created order retains a balance of justice and loving kindness. The larder of creation is not reserved for the economically secure and socially and politically prominent. Notice in the psalms that creation's ultimate hospitable nature is known in justice and generosity.

Matthew's description of the final judgment in chapter 25 alludes to the lifestyle of generosity and sharing that has become second nature for those slated for the reign of heaven. They cannot think of what they did that would be considered worthy of praise! "Aw shucks, it's just what anybody else would have done." And the King will answer them, "Truly, I say to you, as you did it to one of the least of these my brethren, you did it to me." These are the wonders of creation: a hospitable place seeded with such second-nature hospitality.

Discussion and Action

1. Share your lists (and perhaps your art) from the preparation time—meaningful images of God as Creator. In what ways do these images express God's hospitality? How is our hospitality an extension of God's creation?
2. What implications for stewardship of the earth do you find in our faith in a hospitable God? What is our God-given "dominion" over creation?
3. Guests who have been shown hospitality generally like to return the favor. How are we welcoming God as a guest? A Swedish table grace begins, "Lord of joy, be a guest at our table today." What if God were your dinner guest?
4. In what ways can the music in your church's services of worship be hospitable or inhospitable to the strangers in your midst?
5. If possible, play a recording of "Creation" from *God's Trombones* by James Weldon Johnson. Perhaps someone in the group could memorize it and offer it in a worship service of your church.

4

Restore Us Again!: Songs of Lament
Psalm 13; Psalm 22; Psalm 85

> *While life's dark maze I tread,*
> *And griefs around me spread,*
> *be thou my guide.*
> *Bid darkness turn to day,*
> *wipe sorrow's tears away,*
> *nor let me ever stray from thee aside.*
>
> —Ray Palmer, 1830 (HWB 565, CH 576)

Personal Preparation

1. Read Psalm 13. What do you think was happening to and in the psalmist?
2. Read Psalm 22 and look for phrases quoted in the story of Jesus' crucifixion (Mark 15). Note how lament and trust go hand in hand.
3. In private, try "moaning" a spiritual: "Were You There?" (CH 198, HWB 257) and "I Want Jesus to Walk with Me" (CH 627, HWB 439). Imagine the pain and injustice that birthed this musical style. Imagine that your only hope for freedom is in the way you sing. The capacity to *feel* this music is more important than artistic technique.
4. Identify a song/hymn that speaks to you on each of the four following topics. Sing and pray them as you study and meditate: (a) pain and suffering; (b) feeling abandoned by God; (c) trust in God; (d) renewal of relationship with God.

Understanding

"I feel so angry when you don't show up when you say you will!" "I'm out of my mind with worry . . . " "I'm so scared." "Things are closing in . . ." "I *needed* you." These are I-messages, today's version of acceptable communication. A full I-message states one's feelings, describes offending behavior, and relates tangible ways one has been affected. This form of communication can be very effective, *but* a confrontation of this sort usually works only if you want to maintain and strengthen your relationship with the person who is bugging you.

A relationship of intimacy gives healthy freedom to speech. Is it not true that within your few truly intimate relationships, little, if anything, cannot be said? What is usually uncomfortable, unmentionable, or unthinkable can be spoken. Just so with God and the psalmist—when the relationship was intimate, there were no holds barred in either praise or complaint.

Although laments form a significant portion of the Psalms (and are found elsewhere in the Bible as well), they are often neglected in lectionaries and liturgies. Perhaps because we don't understand them, western Christians have not reaped the benefits of the lament tradition as well as they might. How can one express anger and love at the same time? I think of scenes in the movie *Moonstruck,* in which a family fights and yells at each other one minute and hugs one another the next. How can these feelings co-exist?

The laments of the Old Testament Psalms give us a clue. They are the I-messages of the Israelites to God: they state the psalmist's strong feelings, they describe God's offending behavior, and they list tangible results.

The psalms of lament have a general structure:

A brief **invocation**, often including an intimate address to God
> An invocation calls on God. In this context, however, it is not a polite tap at the door, but a verbal grabbing of God's shoulders—"Listen up!" These are not politically correct questions, but pleas to an intimate "you." They are not questions raised in guilt and penitence, but in great anxiety.

The **complaint**, revealing to God how desperate the situation is (often poetically overstated)
> In *The Message of the Psalms,* Old Testament scholar Walter Brueggemann insists that to pray such a psalm is a bold act of faith. Taking our complaints to God helps us to be real, not phony, for

disorder in our lives is a proper subject of discourse with God. Nothing is out of bounds in an intimate relationship; indeed, Brueggemann asserts, all parts of life must be put into speech and addressed to God.

A petition, asking God to act decisively with compassion and justice
In boldly imperative terms, the lament petitions God to pay attention and correct the situation. Psalm 13 (vv. 3-4) is a good example of a petition. It has a simple, clear structure (vv. 1-2, lament; vv. 3-4, petition; vv. 5-6, thanksgiving). This psalm seems to be the prayer of a gravely ill person, who is perhaps even panicked, since death, for Israelites, was thought to end one's active relationship with God. Even though healing was a goal for this writer, the primary concern of this and all of the lamenting psalmists was the *righting of relationship with God*. If death were to come, there would be no chance for that. It is important to get it right in life.

A statement of **trust**, believing God has heard and will act
Scholars are not sure why the psalms of lament *suddenly* break into songs of trust and praise. Perhaps they relate a personal spiritual experience, or maybe portions of some psalms were written over a long period of time. Regardless, if there were no element of trust, there could be no lament, no petition. Even when we're angry or feeling abandoned, we must have *some* trust that God will hear our lament, or there would be no point in complaining.

Praise and commitment, **pledging** to pay all vows
The psalmist's change of attitude culminates in expressions of trust and praise and pledges. One of the cartoons in the *Baby Blues* strip depicts Mom's head bursting with prayers and promises as young Zoe flies off a chair: "Please don't let her fall on her head! . . . If she's not hurt, I swear I'll never yell at her again." Next frame: "I'm all right, Mommy." And from her prone position, Mom lifts her eyes and says, "I suppose you're going to hold me to that promise?"

Meanwhile, we see in the New Testament how Jesus turns to psalms in his own anguish and need. Psalm 22 has been called the "fifth gospel account of the crucifixion." In the lament we see Jesus' suffering most clearly. Can we imagine the grief of the One he calls "Abba"?

Psalm 22:18
*They divide my garments among them,
and for my clothing they cast lots.*

Mark 15:24
*And they crucified him,
and divided his clothes among them,
casting lots to decide what each should take.*

Psalm 22:1
*My God, my God,
why have you forsaken me?*

Mark 15:34
*At three o'clock Jesus cried out with a loud voice,
"Eloi, Eloi, lema sabachthani?"
which means, "My God, my God, why have you forsaken me?"*

The third verse of Thomas Troeger's hymn "How Long, O God, How Long" (CH 642) picks up this Gospel theme, taking its cue from the fact that Jesus himself used it on the cross. This and other songs less "lamentful" express for us the ultimate concern for right relationship with God: "Day by day" (HWB 569, CH 599), "I Need Thee Every Hour" (HWB 555, CH 578).

The image of placing our hands in God's hands arises time and time again. A timeless favorite dating to the 1860s is "He Leadeth Me" (HWB 599, CH 545). Perhaps the most famous is the beloved "Precious Lord, Take My Hand" (HWB 575, CH 628), written in the early 1930s by blues/jazz/gospel musician Thomas A. Dorsey after the death of his wife and baby in childbirth. Writing this song was the beginning of the healing of his spirit, the function of lament.

The psalms of lament acknowledge that life is in God's hands. They are sometimes raw, full of emotion. Their intensity may frighten or put off some of us western moderns who tend to reserve such expression for the privacy of our rooms. But lament is also communal, because life (and death) happen to whole communities. Psalm 85 is a good example of a communal lament. Since there is no mention of a king or a temple, perhaps this psalm comes from early in the return of the exile, when memory of the punishment of the exile is fresh and the task of rebuilding looks daunting. In this psalm the statement of trust is especially graphic (vv. 10-11): "Steadfast love and faithfulness will meet; righteousness and peace will kiss each other. Faithfulness will spring up from the ground, and righteousness will look down from the sky." As powerful as sorrow and anger are, this picture of restoration—the ground and goal of lament—envelops complaint in embrace from above, below, and around.

Discussion and Action

1. The Japanese poet Kenji Miyazawa has said that we must embrace pain and burn it as fuel for our journey. Author Matthew Fox has said that facing pain makes courage the most essential virtue on the spiritual journey. Do you agree? Why?
2. How do you face times "when bad things happen to good people"? How do you respond when the pain of life is great? How do you lament? Can you tell about it? How would you *like* to respond?
3. Sing several of the songs that express the pain of life and the hope and trust of your faith. How is singing your faith different from mere verbal description?
4. Write a communal lament. It could be about local acts of violence or other injustices, an ecological abuse, or any appropriate topic. Review the lament pattern and use it; perhaps try also the pattern of Hebrew poetry (see ch. 1), which pairs lines of similar thought (such as "A, and what's more, B!").
5. Sing together "My Life Flows On" (HWB 580, CH 619).

5

Songs of Thanksgiving
Psalm 136; Psalm 107; Colossians 3:17

> *Now thank we all our God*
> *with heart and hands and voices,*
> *who wondrous things has done,*
> *in whom this world rejoices,*
> *who, from our mother's arms,*
> *has bless'd us on our way*
> *with countless gifts of love,*
> *and still is ours today.*
>
> —Martin Rinchart, 1636.
> Tr. by Catherine Winkworth (HWB 86, CH 715)

Personal Preparation

1. Read aloud the scripture texts for the session. Identify the common refrain in the two psalms.
2. Each day list one thing for which you are especially thankful. In prayer, focus on the many facets of this one thanksgiving.
3. Each day this week look for a way to express your gratitude to someone—and do it! Be open to saying "random words of kindness."

Understanding

"Practicing the presence of God" has taken a specific new turn in my life in the past few years. In my attempt to integrate body, mind, and soul into a meaningful whole, I have come to see that every waking moment is to be lived in response to God. As a result, I have a heightened awareness of my senses and a new lifestyle of thankfulness. This heightened attention to God's presence is worship in the broadest sense.

Songs of Thanksgiving

The abiding theme of the psalter is God's saving grace. The songs of thanksgiving offer thanks for what God has done to rescue an individual or the community. These songs respond to such acts of deliverance as healing from illness, rescue from an enemy or, more generally, rescue from trouble. At the heart of these songs is the story of God's deliverance. The story of the exodus became the touchstone for the wonderful works of God and for the people's gratefulness and praise. Scholars believe that the oldest song in the Bible is the exodus thanksgiving song of Moses and Miriam (Exod. 15:1, 21).

Psalm 136 is a congregational litany. There is a regular heartbeat in the refrain, "for his steadfast love endures forever." The Hebrew for "steadfast love" is the important word *hesed*, which implies a blood relationship. More broadly, it can mean strength, or a strong sense of loyalty, such as would be assumed with kinship. In other words, Psalm 136 has as its refrain an acknowledgment that kinship between Israel and God cannot be broken.

Thematically this psalm begins with God's universal grace in creation (vv. 4-9); becomes very specific in the exodus, the wanderings in the desert, and the conquest of Canaan (vv. 10-22); then is updated to the present ("remembered us," "rescued us"); and concludes on a universal note again ("gives food to all," "the God of heaven"). It is the Great Hallel, or song of praise, sung on the morning of every sabbath.

Psalm 107 is also for communal thanks, probably sung originally in gratitude for restoration after the Babylonian exile. In the psalm we see four distinct occasions on which thank offerings were appropriate: safe passage through the desert (vv. 4-9), release from prison (vv. 10-16), recovery from serious illness (vv. 17-22), and surviving a storm at sea (vv. 23-32). These are all situations far beyond the management of humans alone. They require a God of wonders, a God bearing *hesed*. According to Carroll Stuhlmueller, this psalm "embraces the totality of life; it reaches into the most desperate moments of our existence, and enables us to realize that God's steadfast love—the bond of love and blood which unites us as kinspersons—embraces and cares for the tender roots of our lives."

In a single verse, Paul defines a lifestyle of thankfulness and recommends it to the Colossians (3:17): "And whatever you do, in word or deed, do everything in the name of the Lord Jesus, giving thanks to God the Father through him." Giving thanks is also mentioned in the two previous verses, compounding the emphasis: "And be thankful . . . sing psalms, hymns and spiritual songs to God." Biblical gratitude centers on the grace of God in everyday life—healing, deliverance from enemies, a good harvest—and grace of cosmic proportions: creation, the Exodus, and Jesus Christ. It is not constrained by time and is not nearly so dependent on a quick-fix response from God as we tend to require today. Because we don't always feel thankful, it takes training to keep ourselves alert to God's presence in our lives. More than an attitude or an emotion, gratitude is, admittedly, a difficult discipline. Henri Nouwen has written an entire book about the subject (called *Gratitude*, of course!). He acknowledges that gratitude "challenges me to face the painful moments . . . and gradually discover in them the pruning hands of God. . . ." The operative word here is *gradual*. A discipline does not happen overnight.

A lifestyle of Christian thankfulness is leavened by many "small" thanksgivings. I'd like to suggest eight:

1. Accepting every part of life as a gift from God: the good, with humility; the bad, as potential for blessing. This includes gifts such as talents, family of origin, material possessions, education, experience, sexuality, and the list goes on indefinitely.
2. Treating God's gifts with awe and curiosity. Come as a little child!
3. Maintaining a mind-set of abundance instead of scarcity (no more "poor me" games).
4. Receiving God's gifts appreciatively and being a steward of them as a co-creator with God.
5. Remembering who God remembers—"he regards the lowly" (Ps. 138:6).
6. Giving—this is the nature of grace, to bring joy to God and to one another.
7. Expressing thanks—as Meister Eckhart, the thirteenth-century German theologian and mystic, says, "If the only prayer you say in your life is 'thank you,' that would suffice."
8. Singing—music is a soul language that expresses depth of feeling that cannot be put into words. According to writer Wendy Wright, the early Christians "knew that the Psalms contained within their verses all the possibilities of human experience. To sing the Psalms was to gather up the entire fabric of one's experience and offer it as a sacrifice of praise."

In our Judeo-Christian tradition, singing "psalms and hymns and spiritual songs with thankfulness in your hearts to God" is central to worship. Though I have discovered that thanksgiving is indeed pervasive in scripture and hymnody, it is not as explicit as I had expected. Specifi-

Songs of Thanksgiving 23

cally, I would hope for more expression of thanksgiving in hymns for communion, "the Great Thanksgiving" itself.

In the wonderful proliferation of new hymns in the past thirty years, have you found hymns of thanksgiving that are particularly meaningful to you? Jaroslav J. Vajda's "God of the Sparrow" (CH 70) is a new favorite of mine. It asks unanswerable questions about how we thank God for the wonders of life and creation. That sense of indescribable awe described in Vajda's hymn is not even lost on Hollywood. There is a moment in the 1997 movie *Contact* when astronomer Ellie Arroway experiences a visual feast in a time-warped space adventure. She is overwhelmed and says, "They should have sent a poet."

Discussion and Action

1. Identify personal characteristics and actions that point to a lifestyle of thanksgiving.
2. Why is being thankful such an integral part of being Christian? Why and in what specific ways can we be thankful in the down sides of life?
3. Would you agree with Meister Eckhart that "thank you" is the most important prayer of all?
4. Try some psalm singing or chanting, a longstanding tradition in Christendom that has been mostly lost in American Protestantism. If you have access to *The Lutheran Book of Worship* (Augsburg Fortress), you will find the Psalms marked for singing or reading responsively.
5. Sing the songs of thanksgiving that group members brought from their Suggestions for Sharing and Prayer.

6

Here Is My Servant, My Chosen: Servant Songs
Isaiah 42:1-4; 49:1-6; 50:4-11; 52:13–53:12

> *O lead me, Lord, that I may lead*
> *the wand'ring and the wav'ring feet.*
> *O feed me, Lord, that I may feed*
> *thy hung'ring ones with manna sweet.*
>
> —Frances R. Havergal, 1872 (HWB 499)

Personal Preparation

1. As you read the Servant Songs in the Isaiah passages for this session, list characteristics of the servant.
2. This week, pretend you're an undercover reporter doing a story on servant-acts. Clip articles, gather pictures, observe those around you for occasions great and small when servant-acts work for God's will.
3. Listen to the passion portions of Handel's *The Messiah*.

Understanding

Who comes to mind when you read the following description by Christian educator James Fowler? "They have the kind of vision and commitment that seems to free them for a passionate yet detached spending of themselves in love. They are devoted to overcoming divisions, oppression and violence. They are grounded as if in oneness with the power and being of God" (*Weaving the New Creation*).

Can you see yourself in it? Do you know someone in your congregation or in your town? Do you think of someone famous?

This description at best identifies few people in our experience. In Fowler's extensive study and stories of seven basic stages of faith, this is the seventh, which he terms "universalizing" faith. At this stage, a person has nearly completed the process of decentering from self, where we all began as infants.

Fowler and his colleagues name several people who apparently moved into a truly universalizing stage of faith—Gandhi, John Woolman, Sojourner Truth, Dorothy Day, Thomas Merton, Martin Luther King, Jr. They seem to have truly seen and valued life through God's perspective rather than their own.

The Servant Songs of Isaiah are about a person who embodies this kind of completely selfless love or "universalizing faith." God chooses this person for a special task in words that are akin to a confirmation or ordination ceremony. The identity of the servant is ambiguous. Christians have identified the servant as Christ; Jewish readers tend to see a reference to the community of God's people, Israel. This servant is gentle and nonviolent, strong and peaceful in the face of persecution, steadfast of soul and resolute of spirit. We are told the servant will undergo scandal and loss of friends and will finally be vindicated—but not soon enough to save his/her/their life.

Isaiah's task, like that of other Israelite prophets, was to deliver the news of how God was currently working in the world. But in contrast to other prophets whose work consisted of "public and impassioned announcement of God's condemnation of Israel," that of the present servant would be the quiet proclamation of God's universal rule, which would bring comfort to the exiles. The second part of Isaiah focuses on the reality that servanthood would result in suffering, humiliation, and death for the sake of the world's salvation—being "a light to the nations."

It didn't take long for Jesus' followers to identify him with the Servant Songs of Isaiah. The Ethiopian eunuch was reading from Isaiah 53 when Philip witnessed to the eunuch and baptized him. Paul quoted Isaiah 52:15 in describing Christ's mission to the Gentiles (Rom. 15:21). Like Jesus himself, the writers of the New Testament were well schooled in the teaching method of integration. Wherever possible, they connected Hebrew scripture to their writings, giving them substance, credence, and authority, hanging them on a common thread of salvation history. Jesus' willing suffering and his blamelessness were quickly associated with the prophecies and songs of Isaiah.

Centuries later, one of the most beloved of musical works—Handel's *The Messiah*—drew heavily upon the Servant Songs. Recall these familiar passages from Isaiah 53, used in "Part 2, Passion and Resurrection": *He was despised and rejected of men; a man of sorrows, and acquainted with grief. . . . Surely he hath borne our griefs, and carried our sorrows; He was wounded for our transgressions; He was bruised for our iniquities; the chastisement of our peace was upon Him. And with his stripes we are healed. All we like sheep have gone astray; we have turned every one to his own way; and the Lord has laid on Him the iniquity of us all.*

The Messiah was composed from the libretto of Charles Jennens, a pompous man according to those who knew him. He has been quoted as saying that Handel made a "fine entertainment" of his work, though not as good as it could have been. Handel is reputed to have responded, "I should be sorry if I only entertained them; I wished to make them better." Indeed, Handel used the oratorio for numerous benefit concerts, his favorite being the hospital for homeless and maltreated children.

The Messiah puts together Old Testament prophecy with the New Testament account of Jesus' life and Passion, just as the early church saw Jesus as a fulfillment of prophecy. *The Messiah* has us looking at Jesus through Isaiah's eyes. Jesus led the servant life, as priest and author Daniel Berrigan says, by how he waited and listened, observed and debated, healed and conveyed hope with humor, told stories that invited people to think. Jesus exemplified love, which, according to author M. Scott Peck, seeks growth at all times, even through pain. The avoidance of pain is the road to ill health.

But is this call to servanthood for everyone? Is true servanthood reserved for only those saintly ones who seem ultra-inspired? It reminds me of the story of how, once, when frustrated with her husband's keen sense of righteousness, the wife of Mohandas K. Gandhi cried out, "But some of us don't even *want* to be as good as you!" While many of us admire such dedication and selflessness in servanthood, how many of us can recognize when the time is ripe for *us*? How many can overcome the fears?

Certainly God calls us to be servants and to set aside our own comforts for the healing of others. Certainly we are stirred by hymns that call us to serve, to bear one another's burdens, to live lightly in the world, to be generous to a fault. But the Servant Songs of Isaiah are not where God does the calling. They are a true prophecy, telling it how it is.

Servanthood is a mark of the Christian life. Daniel Berrigan describes what characteristics of servanthood might include for us in our time: being teachable and being a listener; embodying passion for justice and telling the truth; rehabilitating the prisoner, stoop workers, and illegal aliens; being peaceful in the face of provocation; keeping the faith under duress; refusing to take refuge in unjust laws; being attentive to both the word of God and the machinations of the world. We are to ask questions; shoulder the burdens of life, vocation, and fidelity rather than thrusting them on others; acknowledge our complicity in sin and respond with action on behalf of others; be scornfully silent in response to illegitimate questions and speak when truth can be conveyed; know the consequences of faithful actions and stand by them.

The Suffering Servant not only exemplifies profound, self-sacrificing faith; this Servant image is also a means by which the prophet calls the covenant people to understand their own exile in a sacrificial way—they could be God's Servant Israel as a "light to the nations." The Servant Songs explain how God is working in people who are called to give their very lives to divine love. Hearing stories of such people renews my faith in God, and that is the intention of the songs.

But do not suppose we are off the hook in terms of being called to serve. Our songs are full of reminders that challenge our complacency: "Here I Am, Lord" (HWB 395, CH 452); "The Church of Christ in Every Age" (HWB 403, CH 475); "Will You Let Me Be Your Servant" (HWB 307, CH 490).

Discussion and Action

1. Think of the "radical" Christians you know. Do they exhibit a "universalizing" (in Fowler's terms), selfless faith?
2. When have you experienced suffering as redemptive?
3. Can you find servant themes in spirituals? How does the suffering servant image affect slaves and the oppressed? Do we similarly feel this way about voluntary poverty?
4. Describe your "growing edges" of servanthood. What do you feel called to do or explore that seems risky, yet important for your faith development?

7

My Soul Magnifies the Lord: Nativity Songs

Luke 1:46-55, Mary's Song, the "Magnificat"
Luke 1:67-79, Zechariah's Song, the "Benedictus"
Luke 2:29-32, Simeon's Song, the "Nunc Dimittis"

Personal Preparation

1. Read the songs of Mary, Zechariah, and Simeon noted above. Summarize what each is saying in a sentence or two. Memorize one of the songs.
2. Read Luke 1–2:40. Confining yourself to *this reading alone*, write a list of what you know about angels. Draw a line under your list, and then continue it as you read Advent and Christmas hymn texts that mention angels.
3. Browse through the Advent hymns in your hymnal. Look for the language and references to Old Testament scriptures. Check the hymnal's scripture index for references to this week's nativity songs in scripture.

Understanding

Collected in the Gospel of Luke are the jubilant songs that Mary, Zechariah, and Simeon sang to welcome the Messiah. Their music became the golden oldies of all Christmas carols. Like all golden oldies, they have a certain timeless quality about them. People have loved Mary's Song, the Magnificat ("My soul magnifies the Lord"), in every age. But it's not a faded glory or romanticizing of the past that makes these songs so universal; it's that they sing of all time, past, present, and future in one moment.

The coming of Jesus is the fulcrum of history. Everything before him points to his coming, and everything after him is the result of his reconciling role for the world. The moment he arrives in the present, the past is vindicated and the future is fulfilled. For every age, that moment is now. We experience his reconciling love as a moment of change that closes out the old age and ushers in a whole new way of thinking and being in the world.

The past is represented in the songs of Mary, Zechariah, and Simeon through the prophets, who are quoted eight times. For instance, Zechariah quotes Malachi 3:1, saying that John will be the prophet who comes in advance of the Anointed One to prepare the way. Simeon's praise for our God who sends the revelation even to the Gentiles (Luke 2:32) rings like Isaiah 49:6 in which God's message is promised to people at the ends of the earth, not just the twelve tribes of Israel. For God's people, the past is made up of the march toward fulfillment of the promise to Abraham and to all nations, which Mary, Zechariah, and Simeon would have heard rehearsed over and over in the Jewish community. Even on the brink of a new day, the longstanding message of the past surfaces readily in their memories.

Now they stand at the present. The promise is no longer just ahead or just beyond their grasp. The promise that the prophets told is here. He is real. He has a name—Jesus, Light of the world, Savior. He has a mission—turn the world upside down; bring down the powerful and raise up the lowly; prepare the way, reconciling people to God; and make light shine in the darkness.

Perhaps the most remarkable aspect of time in these songs, however, is the future. Here the future collapses into the present. Mary sings of God's mercy that will be accomplished in the as yet unborn Jesus as though it is already done: "He has shown strength . . . he has scattered the proud. . . ." Hannah's song in 1 Samuel 2 about the gift of her son, Samuel, is similar to Mary's, but God's saving action is described as a future event there (1 Sam. 2:9-10). Bible scholar Fred Craddock says that Mary's song speaks with such assurance that God will do what is promised that it uses a verb tense in Greek that expresses timelessness and truth.

Magnificat. The story of the annunciation, the encounter of Mary with the angel Gabriel, has sometimes brought us a picture of a sweet, gentle, acquiescent young woman, the perfect, loving mother for a cherubic baby boy. The story does say that Mary identifies herself as God's servant and that she will accept her "assignment." After all, if what she is hearing is true, it is the ultimate dream of every Hebrew mother that the child she bears could be the Deliverer.

Being humble doesn't mean that Mary willingly accepted her "station in life," however. Her song would have been enough to get her jailed in some societies. Mary was humble not so much because she took whatever God handed her, but because her trust in God allowed her to be strong through the whole ordeal of being the mother of a misunderstood Christ. True to Old Testament style, her words portray future acts of God as already accomplished. It is that strange paradox of the reign of God that it can be "already but not yet."

Mary's song is almost completely devoted to the blessing she has received and that which God will bring through her to the poor, powerless, and oppressed of the world. Indeed, it was a foolish thing in the world's eyes to send a baby and proclaim him a king, to choose a skeptical, small-town priest and his wife, a peasant girl and her working-class fiancé, and shepherds to herald a new age. Here, as in much of Luke's Gospel, God works in and through average people and their faithful community. It is faith, not political power, that puts one in position to be used for God's purpose.

Benedictus. In the tradition of Hebrew prophecy, Zechariah's song alludes to a number of Old Testament passages to show how the events he is relating today fit a pattern of God's activity among creation. In Luke 1:69, God is become "a horn of salvation" (Greek); an animal's strength is in its horn, so God is a horn in this act of salvation. And where the Magnificat lays out economic and political reversal, the Benedictus underscores the ethical transformation brought on by the Messiah (E. Earle Ellis). In verse 76, Zechariah's emphasis switches from Messiah to his own son, John, as the forerunner, then broadens again in verse 78, heralding a new name for Messiah as "dawn," or yet more poetic, "dayspring."

Zechariah, too, prophesied in terms of peace. He was not ready to die but ready to live: "that we, being delivered from the hand of our enemies, might serve him without fear . . ." (1:74b).

While Zechariah's and Mary's songs are directed specifically to the community of Israel, Simeon's song expands outward and forward to Jesus' ministry and the church's mission to all peoples.

Nunc Dimittis. Simeon's song is one of recognition, of a man singularly attuned to God's active spirit. The song takes up a theme that will later be elaborated in the Gospel of Luke: The gift of salvation, messianic deliverance, is for both Gentiles and Jews. Another radical speech. When Simeon says that he is ready to "depart in peace" (2:29), we have no clue as to his age, but we are given insight in his choice of the word *death* which, according to Craddock, is the same language used when freeing a slave (*Luke*). "Free at last! Free at last! Thank God Almighty, I'm free at last!"

The songs of Mary, Zechariah, and Simeon in Luke are unique among the four Gospels, and they serve as a descriptive framework for the entire book of Luke. There is speculation that Luke borrowed these songs from early Christian liturgies and that Zechariah's song may have been circulated among the followers of John. Luke was not so much concerned to *prove* the messiahship of Jesus as he was to *show* what it was like. Songs do that. They are emotive, they are poetic, they touch people at a level untapped by logical theory. Luke also probably realized that music and song, while they are not in themselves doctrine, do *support* doctrine. One of the easiest ways to imbibe a concept is to sing it. Mary's, Simeon's, and Zechariah's songs were full of the radical, promising nature of this extraordinarily ordinary birth. Their theme matched the book's themes of an authentically divine and radical reign that came among both Jews and Gentiles.

These three songs of joy and prophecy are commonly referred to by their opening words in Latin: *Magnificat* ("magnify"), *Benedictus* ("blessed") and *Nunc Dimittis* ("Now lettest . . . depart"). They have enjoyed diverse musical settings and are sung regularly in the Roman Catholic and Anglican liturgies. Your hymnal probably includes settings of one or two.

About a dozen years ago my congregation called a new pastor who asked us that first year to take the season of Advent more seriously than was our custom. Specifically, he chose to use no Christmas carols until Christmas Sunday itself. It was part of the Advent waiting to confine ourselves to Advent songs and save the birth of Christ for the birthday. Like many in the congregation, I missed singing carols throughout December.

I don't remember exactly when I became aware that my attitude toward Advent had changed, and even been revolutionized. No longer was Advent a time of full-speed-ahead frenzy to get it done by Christmas, but year by year it became more deeply a time of reflection on what it means to wait in hope for the salvation of the world and also experience reconciliation as something that is already accomplished. I became more acutely aware of what was happening in the world due to human sin, a world untouched by the news of the "sweet little Jesus child." I slowed my pace, I cut back on shopping, and my annual Christmas song became a richer time of waiting and celebrating. As my lifestyle allowed me more openness to the waiting, pregnant spirit of Advent, I became more like Mary, Zechariah, and Simeon—an ordinary person whose normal life, when overlaid with growing faith, puts me in position to be used for God's purposes. It's truly exciting!

Discussion and Action

1. What Advent/Christmas stories in your life tell of the working of the Holy Spirit?
2. Expand your repertoire of nativity songs. Look for the themes of Mary, Zechariah, and Simeon, such as God's covenant and promises, God's mercies, reversals of fortune, peace and justice, and the salvation story for all humanity.
3. Talk about Advent/Christmas traditions in your various households. How do these traditions enhance or negate the themes in the songs of Mary, Zechariah, and Simeon? Challenge yourselves to critique some Advent/Christmas traditions that do *not* fit the spirit of the songs.

8

The Greatest of These: Hymns of Love
1 Corinthians 13

. . . and the greatest of these is love.

—Apostle Paul

Personal Preparation

1. Read 1 Corinthians 13 and write a definition of love. Try limiting it to five words or less.
2. Keep a diary this week on your struggle to define love and your experiences of trying to live by its ideals.
3. Memorize "The Gift of Love" (CH 526) or "Holy Spirit, Gracious Guest" (HWB 542).

Understanding

Think back to the last few times you spoke the word *love*. Did you say to someone, "I love you"? Did the word slip out casually, "I'd love to go!" Did you quote "The love of money is the root of all evil"? Did you sing a hymn such as "I Love Thy Kingdom, Lord" (HWB 308) or "When Love Is Found" (HWB 623, CH 499)?

North Americans are growing up starved for knowledge about love. Our culture has isolated a God-given capacity for *eros* (or romantic love) from all other relationships. *Eros* is celebrated, perhaps even worshiped, in a way that does not leave room for deep friendship or love of family. Popular songs especially tend to give a picture of erotic love that sacrifices everything to some ideal object of desire. The *eros* of popular culture often values passion above meaning and mistakes obsession for real relationship.

Romantic love has always been a chief topic of popular songs, and sex (*eros*) is increasingly the unambiguous, or not so ambiguous, focus. Pop music continually redefines age-old confusions about love, as in "What's Love Got to Do with It" (sung by Tina Turner).

Perhaps the most famous ode to love is the passage from 1 Corinthians, read at nearly every wedding I've ever attended. The thirteenth chapter, while not a hymn, is a poetic statement of love. If it *were* music, it would have been Paul's "greatest hit." But in context, it's not about romantic love (*eros*) at all.

This letter was written to the contentious church at Corinth regarding a dispute over speaking in tongues. Some members believed that the highest manifestation of the Holy Spirit was in *glossolalia*, or ecstatic speaking in tongues. Surely it must have looked like a powerful possession by the Spirit to have even one's speech taken over by God. The church at Corinth was made up mostly of Gentiles who were what we would now call "lower income" and "blue collar," hard-working people with little or no social status, who had responded to the grace of God. They were surrounded by a pagan culture deeply immersed in sensuality for its own sake, and the temptations to worship *eros* must have been great. In his first letter, Paul presents them with a different view of the kind of love that drives healthy relationships.

Paul's "love chapter" is not meant to stand alone. It is part of a larger essay about the kind of community the family of God should be. In chapter 12 Paul uses the analogy of the human body to show the relationship of Christians to Christ and to one another, and the scene is set for the "more excellent way."

Paul does not identify love as a spiritual gift; it is in a category by itself. *Agape* is the Greek word for the self-giving kind of love we associate with God (as in "God is love," 1 John 4:8b). According to Bible scholar William Baird, "Faith is something we *do*, hope is something we *have*; love belongs to the being of *God*." Love is more important than wisdom, theological correctness, or charismatic gifts.

When Christians proclaimed "God is love," they were not putting an esoteric subject on the table for discussion. Rather, they were interpreting their experience of Jesus as love in the flesh—incarnated—a love that continued to be experienced through the presence of the Holy Spirit: "But God proves [not *proved*] his love for us in that while we still were sinners Christ died for us" (Rom. 5:8).

M. Scott Peck, in his book about love, *The Road Less Traveled*, defines love as "the will to extend one's self for the purpose of nurturing one's own or another's spiritual growth." Peck's definition highlights the response nature of love. While human love is a gift of the Holy Spirit to us, it is also our gift to the Holy Spirit and to the spirit of others and to ourselves. So while Paul talks about how love manifests itself—patience, kindness, humility, etc.—Peck focuses on the hard work and the willful, courageous effort it takes to be "hoping, believing, enduring all things" day in and day out.

It is my experience also that love takes hard work, courageous and wise effort and commitment to persevere in church life when inevitable conflict arises. Discipline, it has been suggested, is a primary factor in spiritual growth. Have you ever thought about why prayer, meditation, journaling, and other activities to feed the soul are termed spiritual *disciplines*? It may be, as Peck believes, that the motive and energy for genuine discipline is love.

I think Paul would agree with Peck's definition of love as it applies to our relationships in the church. Paul's reason for commending comprehensible prophecy over incomprehensible *glossolalia* is that speaking in tongues is a private gift which benefits primarily the speaker, whereas prophecy is for the edification—the spiritual growth—of everyone in the community (1 Cor. 14:2-3).

1 Corinthians 13 has been set to music in a variety of ways; some hymns with the strongest connection include "The Gift of Love" (526 CH) and "Holy Spirit, Gracious Guest" (HWB 542). One of my favorite new hymns is about the hard work and courageous perseverance of love, "Help Us Accept Each Other" (CH 487) by Fred Kaan. This would be a good song to memorize and recall "at the blowing of the still." To "blow the still" was a shipboard emergency signal. It called for everyone to stop and calmly think through the best course of action before moving. In his letter, Paul "blows the still" for the contentious Corinthians. There are times in life when we need to "blow the still" and think through how love would have us react.

Discussion and Action

1. Those who wish may share definitions of love. List some concrete ways of expressing individual and congregational love within the church, to the wider public, and to the global community.
2. Are there any situations in your congregation for which it might be a good idea to "blow the still" and consider how love would have us react?

3. Develop a litany that names some of the things we allow to take precedence over love. The refrain might be something like "But it is love which binds us to God and to one another."
4. Sing "Help Us Accept Each Other" (CH 487). What does it suggest about embodying love in the context of your congregation's worship?
5. Sing songs celebrating love in the Christian community. How about some old favorite camp songs? Some from my "era" include "The Magic Penny," "If I Had a Hammer," "Pass It On" (CH 477), "I Am the Light of the World" (CH 469), and "They'll Know We Are Christians by Our Love" (CH 494). Some of these now have their place in the hymnal along with "For the Beauty of the Earth" (ch 56, HWB 89), "I Come with Joy" (CH 420, HWB 459), "Love Came Down at Christmas" (HWB 208), "There Are Many Gifts" (HWB 304), "Holy Spirit, Storm of Love" (HWB 132), "What Wondrous Love Is This" (CH 200, HWB 530), and "When Love Is Found" (CH 499, HWB 623). What are your favorite songs of Christian love?

9

The Image of the Invisible God: Hymns of Faith
Colossians 1:15-20; Philippians 2:5-11

> *O Love of God, how strong and true,*
> *eternal and yet ever new,*
> *uncomprehended and unbought,*
> *beyond all knowledge and all thought.*
>
> —Horatius Bonar, 1861(HWB 326)

Personal Preparation

1. Prepare for the role play in Colossae (see Discussion and Action) by planning how you would answer each question.
2. Choose one image of Jesus Christ that is particularly meaningful to you. Look for artistic interpretations and/or prepare one yourself.
3. With your image of Jesus in mind, make a list of ways you see yourself through this same lens. For example, one African Christian says Jesus is the Good Shepherd because "he's the only one who can keep us all together." How, then, might your ministry be one of helping people communicate with each other?

Understanding

These two Christ hymns in Colossians and Philippians are truly cosmic. They are both setting Christ up as the be-all and end-all of the cosmos—not just of earth, but of heaven and the underworld.

One of the intriguing possibilities in the story of the church at Colossae is that this hymn (Col. 1:15-20), which may already have been known by the Colossian church prior to receiving this letter, indicates there is dialog with the non-Christian culture. The "new thing" that God has done in Christ needs explanation. Therefore, the hymn is infused with strong Christian language, so there will be no ambiguity as to the centrality of Christ.

Theologian Rudolph Bultmann notes there is evidence here that the author, building on the previous notion that the "body" is the cosmos, with Christ as the "head," applies a new interpretation of the "body" as the church, "thereby giving the church the character of a cosmic entity." Thus the church, with Christ as the head, models what it means for the whole cosmos to be renewed and reconciled. The hymn "O Love of God," by nineteenth-century poet and pastor Horatius Bonar affirms God's love made visible in the natural world and in the reconciliation effected by Christ's death and resurrection.

The Christ hymn of Philippians 2:5-11 is also meant to clarify the "new thing." Amid all the various interpretations of Christ's life, one that seems most heretical is a denial of his willing suffering. According to scholar Jean-Francois Collange, itinerant preachers were giving themselves out as splendid patterns to be copied, but they were in complete contrast to the "wretched appearance of the apostle of the Cross." The Christian community was beginning to look the same as everyone else. Where was its *ousia*, its essence, its character? What made it distinctly Christian? The letter is a reminder: believers are to take the *humility* of Christ as a pattern, and that humility comes before any kind of exaltation. For the Greeks, such humility was no virtue; it was akin to the condition of a slave. It was an attitude lauded in the Old Testament, but in the example of Christ, it finds culmination.

These early faith apologies (explanations) are valuable for study, since they address issues and controversies that are still alive today, albeit in different forms. These hymns may have already been circulating in the Judeo-Christian community before they appeared in these letters, and rightly so. They have within them, like all good hymns, always something more to be discovered.

Alvin C. Porteous, in his book *The Search for Christian Credibility*, suggests that making such apologies, or explanations, is still our task. We must find new images to enrich our faith and to help communicate the message of Christ. He recommends three images:

Jesus as gracious neighbor. Jesus lived a supremely hospitable life. He welcomed the poor and socialized with outcasts. He did the work of a household slave and set an example in washing his disciples' dusty feet. As a portion of another hymn in the New Testament says, this humble "man for others" (as Jesus has been called) "did not count equality with God a thing to be grasped, but emptied himself . . . and became obedient unto death, even death on a cross" (Phil. 2:5-11).

Jesus as revolutionary. Think of the radical nature of Jesus' confrontations of "the Establishment"—breaking the law (healing/helping on the sabbath) and destroying personal property (the moneychangers in the temple). Conflict with authorities over interpretation of the law led to the crucifixion precisely because Jesus was a visionary in a myopic world of fearful legalists.

Invincible pioneer. Jesus led human history to a new future, a new vision of the realm of God. The two hymns in Colossians and Philippians name Jesus as "first," "before," "head," "exalted," "beginning," and in other places he is called the "second Adam" and the "pioneer and perfecter of our faith."

Have you tried putting your beliefs about Christ into words? I find it difficult. Some of the biblical and other older images do not speak to me particularly, and I'm sure much less to people who aren't regular churchgoers: king ("president" in these democratic times?), the Amen (say what?), comforter (goose down or synthetic?). Others images do hold imaginative power to help identify who Christ is for me: friend (an intimate one), teacher (one who knows how to help me grow), servant (like several of the influential women in my life). Truth and love express my highest religious aspirations and are qualities and values fervently desired by seekers in our churches.

It is in the New Testament Christ hymns that poetry and art expressly do theology. Finding christology in hymnody helps us express our faith where words might otherwise fail, and it pushes us to understand and explore the faith stance of other believers, both now and in eras gone before.

Discussion and Action

1. Role play a discussion of two groups in Colossae. Members of one group are Christians; members of the other are Jews who are interested in but wary of the Christians' story and faith. The Jews raise questions such as the following:
    a. What do you mean this Jesus was recognized as the Messiah after he arose from the dead? Where is he now?
    b. What is the "body of Christ" and how is Jesus the head?

      c. You say that Christ is the "firstborn" of all creation. How can that be?
      d. We have heard that you believe reconciliation was the chief purpose of this Messiah who was crucified. Is this true? Why?
      e. Did this Christ believe that Gentiles are part of God's plan of salvation?
2. What responsibilities do we have as the body of Christ to continue the divine creation and reconciliation processes in our time and place?
3. Try your own at expressing your christology in verse, with music. As an example, sing the following verse to the familiar tune of "O Jesus, I Have Promised" (ANGEL'S STORY):

> *To hungry spirits searching for food that satisfies,*
> *a truthful bread is offered for our abundant lives:*
> *Christ Jesus feeds the empty with honesty of soul,*
> *The needy here find welcome and that which makes*
>   *them whole.*

4. Sing Bonar's hymn, "O Love of God" (HWB 326), or have someone play the music softly while others read the stanzas. What is the best musical statement of your faith in Christ?

10

Worthy Is the Lamb: Hymns in Revelation
Revelation 5:9-14; 19:1-8; 21:1-4

Crown him with many crowns, the Lamb upon his throne.
Hark! How the heavenly anthem drowns all music but its own.
Awake, my soul, and sing of him who died for thee,
and hail him as thy matchless King through all eternity.

—Matthew Bridges, 1851 (HWB 116, CH 234)

Personal Preparation

1. Read an introduction to the book of Revelation such as found in *The HarperCollins Study Bible* (NRSV) or Richard Lowery's *Revelation* (Covenant Bible Studies series).
2. Read the hymn text above. If you have time, read the entire Revelation—visualize more than analyze. Take note of the images and phrases that you remember seeing depicted in music or art; look for how the vision calls for Christians to repent and to live.
3. Check your hymnal scripture index and read hymns using imagery from Revelation; can you identify images and phrases taken from Revelation?

Understanding

The key of D is my favorite major key in music. It has such a crisp sound compared to the keys in flats or even C major. Have you noticed there *is* a difference? The key of D was selected by George Frederick Handel for the climactic full choruses in *The Messiah* ("Hallelujah" and "Worthy Is the Lamb"). Mystery and awe begin to swell within me as soon as I hear the instrumentalists striking that first D chord or simple octaves.

The "Hallelujah Chorus" and "Worthy Is the Lamb" in Handel's work come from the hymns or hymnlike sections in the "The Revelation of Jesus Christ, which was given to John" (ch. 5, 11, 19). There are some sixteen sections that are hymnlike in this very poetic, even musical, letter. Many of these were inspired by Jewish and Christian liturgies and have stayed with us, inspiring new musical settings of stirring texts.

Elisabeth Schussler Fiorenza recommends approaching Revelation as you would a work of art. For example, the opening verses of chapter 1 indicate that this letter was to be read aloud in worship at one sitting. This, she says, is essential to understanding and appreciating it, much like listening to a whole symphony and watching for motifs and variations, movement, form, and other aspects of a work of art.

Revelation is apocalyptic literature, which is a practiced style of writing. The clash and clang of cataclysmic events in such writing confuses many people, because they are told it is in an inexplicable code that only a few can decipher. "That's simply not true," says writer Frank Ramirez. "Apocalyptic literature tells the same gospel story as the rest of the Bible in *visual*, almost *video* form. The images come thick and fast and what matters is the impression that all the sound bites, put together, form." Sometimes people get so distracted by the noise and light and strange images of the apocalyptic portions of the Bible that they forget that this is still God's book written for the benefit of God's people.

I highly recommend additional study of Revelation, especially in this millennial time when it is a source of quotations, questions, and confusion. Richard Lowery reminds us in his book *Revelation* that the letter was to give hope to early Christians in Asia who faced uncertainty and persecution. We too can learn from it about living in a miserable world with steadfastness and hope. We will look briefly at three of Revelation's hymns, then conclude by reviewing thematic relationships in the hymns of the Bible that have been the focus of this study.

Three hymns. Revelation 5:9-14 is the vocal homage of the heavenly court: the words of a "new song" for the new era Christ has inaugurated (vv. 9-10), a hymn of a myriad of angels (vv. 11-12), praise of the world (v. 13), and a worshipful "Amen" (v. 14). "Lamb," here as throughout Revelation, refers to the resurrected Christ, a strikingly different image from the one a few verses earlier (5:5), the "Lion" of the tribe of Judah. This hymn pictures the whole cosmos worshiping one God, Creator and Redeemer; for John, to know Christ is to know God.

In Revelation 19:1-8, we find a trio of Hallelujahs—the only place in the New Testament where the word is used. This is another scene of worship—praise for the mighty and victorious acts of God in securing the downfall of "Babylon," the "whore." The recurring imagery of marriage describes the relationship of Christ and the church, or the New Jerusalem—the Lamb and his Bride—an idea that will be further developed in chapter 21. This bride is arrayed in the pure linen of righteous acts, in contrast to the whore's red garment of sin.

Matthew Bridges' hymn text "Crown him with many crowns," above, does not come directly from a Revelation hymn, but it is an elaboration of John's vision of the rider on a pale horse, "and on his head are many diadems" (19:11-12). Bridges and other authors make liberal use of this image of crowns; though the hymn's main image is sprung from just part of one verse, it weaves the full majestic and awesome tone from all of Revelation into the meaning of the crowns.

In Revelation 21:1-4, we are given a glimpse of what heaven on earth will be like: God will be among all the people with salvation and the ending of sorrow. The text of John's Revelation was preserved by the early church as an authentic vision from God. It deserves our best Bible study, even though we struggle to understand in ways that the original hearers would not have had to struggle.

Through the ages people in trouble have sung songs or recited prayers to get them through otherwise inhuman situations: prisoners who sang their faith and thereby converted jailers, people who sang on their way to execution, American slaves who sang spirituals with veiled references to freedom and the way north, music that sustained nonviolent resistance movements in Europe, India, the US, Central America, and South Africa. The songs of Revelation were for John's hearers what music has been for countless other sufferers: a way to ease living for God and a way to die to God.

The themes of the hymns of Revelation are the same as in the other music of the Bible. This final book of the New Testament does not tie up all the loose threads of the Bible; rather, it weaves them with colorful metaphor and simile and projects them toward "the end"—the End that is God. But for us to tie up loose ends, here are some observations about how hymn themes of the Bible are intertwined with those of Revelation.

1. **Hymns in the Bible.** God's people have sung their faith in every era, and God is always at the heart of this musical proclamation. If there is one overarching sub-theme in these hymns,

it is God's help/justice/salvation in time of trouble (Exodus, exile, persecution, poverty).
2. **Hymns of praise.** At the beginning of Revelation, John pronounces a blessing on the faith community that reads the prophecy and lives by it. The community is faithful as it confesses Christ, despite cultural and political pressures to the contrary and as it worships with "Hallelujahs."
3. **Creation hymns.** In Revelation's vision the earth is at the center of God's creation, and the "new heaven" will be on earth in justice and salvation for all people.
4. **Songs of lament.** The Revelation is addressed to believers who may have been in a lamenting mode, not unlike the psalmists in times of trouble. Elements of lament are contained in the complaints and petitions of a persecuted people as well as in statements of trust and praise of God who holds the future and "will wipe away every tear from their eyes."
5. **Songs of thanksgiving.** Whenever the words *thanks* and *thanksgiving* appear in Revelation, they are in the context of worship. This should not surprise us since thanksgiving was the most basic purpose and posture of the Hebrew/Jewish worship.
6. **The Suffering Servant.** The message of Revelation to people under persecution is a word of victory that the Suffering Servant has already paid the price of faithful obedience and is glorified by God. The "new song" (5:9-10) celebrates this worthy Lamb's suffering a violent death, being God's agent in purchasing the freedom of all people, and creating the community of the redeemed.
7. **Nativity songs.** For John, as for Mary, the kingdom of God is already present; like Zechariah, John believes God is working to bring justice; like Simeon, John envisions God's salvation as a gift not only for Israel, but for all people.
8. **The greatest of these is love**. Paul's theme is "love never ends," and John admonishes Asian Christians for just such a sin: ". . . you have abandoned the love you had at first . . . repent, and do the works you did at first" (Rev. 2:4-5). The hymn in chapter 21 (vv. 3-4) promises God's loving presence in sorrow, death, and pain.
9. **"Christ hymns"** quoted in the New Testament epistles may have served as common hymnody for the early churches. The hymns put into words the beliefs of the church and they were endorsed (and perhaps "enhanced") by writers like Paul. As

such they were creedlike and perhaps used as the final court of appeal in local christological questions. The Revelation hymns about Christ do with imagery what the epistle hymns do with careful theology: they pass on the good news of Jesus Christ.

Discussion and Action

1. Imagine yourself in the early Asian church, under pressure to worship Caesar. Choose one of the following options for a faith response and explain your choice: quit the faith, lie, fight the Empire, synthesize your Christianity with the Roman religion and culture, or die bearing witness to Christ.
2. Identify three key strands running through the music of the Bible. How do your ideas compare with others in your group?
3. What is it about music that delivers God's message to us more meaningfully than other ways?
4. Sing some "Revelation" songs. These might include "Alabaré" ("Oh, I Will Praise") (CH 29); "My Lord, What a Morning" (CH 708), "When Peace, Like a River" (HWB 336, CH 561); "Sleepers, Wake" (HWB 188); "Beyond a Dying Sun" (HWB 323); "At the Lamb's High Feast" (HWB 262); "Oh, Holy City Seen of John" (HWB 320); "Come Away to the Skies" (HWB 284).

Suggestions for Sharing and Prayer

This material is designed for covenant groups that spend one hour sharing and praying together, followed by one hour of Bible study. The following suggestions will help relate the group's sharing and prayer time to their study of *Hymns and Songs of the Bible.* Ideally, groups will use this opportunity to share with one another at an increasing depth as the weeks pass. Session-by-session ideas as well as ideas for forming a covenant group are provided in the following pages.

This section was written by Lani Wright, editor of the *Hymnal Companion.* She is also a writer and editor of adult and youth curriculum. Lani resides in Cottage Grove, Oregon.

Forming a Covenant Group

Covenant Expectations

Covenant-making is significant throughout the biblical story. God made covenants with Noah, Abraham, and Moses. Jeremiah speaks about God making a covenant with the people, "written on the heart." In the New Testament, Jesus is identified as the mediator of the new covenant, and the early believers lived out of covenant relationships. Throughout history people have lived in covenant relationship with God and within community.

Christians today also covenant with God and make commitments to each other. Such covenants help believers live out their faith. God's empowerment comes to them as they gather in covenant communities to pray and study, share and receive, reflect and act.

People of the Covenant is a program that is anchored in this covenantal history of God's people. It is a network of covenantal relationships. Denominations, districts or regions, congregations, small groups, and individuals all make covenants. Covenant group members commit themselves to the mission statement, seeking to become more . . .
—biblically informed so they better understand the revelation of God;
—globally aware so they know themselves to be better connected with all of God's world;
—relationally sensitive to God, self, and others.

The Burlap Cross Symbol
The imperfections of the burlap cross, its rough texture and unrefined fabric, the interweaving of threads, the uniqueness of each strand, are elements that are present within the covenant group. The people in the groups are imperfect, unpolished, interrelated with each other, yet still unique beings.

The shape that this collection of imperfect threads creates is the cross, symbolizing for all Christians the resurrection and presence of Christ our Savior. A covenant group is something akin to this burlap cross. It unites common, ordinary people and sends them out again in all directions to be in the world.

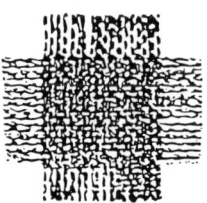

A Litany of Commitment
All:	*We are a people of the covenant; out of our commitment to Christ, we seek to become:*
Group 1:	more biblically informed so we understand better God's revelation;
Group 2:	more globally aware so we know ourselves connected with all of God's people;
Group 1:	more relationally sensitive to God, self, and others.
All:	*We are a people of the covenant; we promise:*
Group 2:	to seek ways of living out and sharing our faith;
Group 1:	to participate actively in congregational life;
Group 2:	to be open to the leading of the Spirit in our lives.
All:	*We are a people of the covenant; we commit ourselves:*
Group 1:	to attend each group meeting, so far as possible;
Group 2:	to prepare through Bible study, prayer, and action;
Group 1:	to share thoughts and feelings, as appropriate;
Group 2:	to encourage each other on our faith journeys.
All:	*We are a people of the covenant.*

Session-by-Session Suggestions
Any study of hymns should include lots of singing! For each of your covenant meetings, bring two or three hymns that relate to the theme of the session; they can be special favorites of yours or one that you'd like to try. Since each person in your covenant group will be doing the same thing, you will need to pick and choose which ones you actually have time to sing or play. If, during the prayer and sharing time you spend

more time singing than you do talking or writing litanies, that's fine! Through the singing, you will be sharing, you will be praying together, and perhaps you will also be expanding your experience of God.

1. Sing Aloud to God Our Strength

❏ Share with the group the "crisis" hymn or stanza that came to mind as you did your personal preparation for this session. What are the associations you make with this hymn or song that especially express your faith?

❏ Without using hymnals, have people take turns starting a hymn they know by heart. Others join in as they pick up the tune. During this memory songfest, start a list of hymns you already know by heart. You may be surprised at how many you know! Keep going as long as you can!

❏ Do a choral reading of a psalm (100 or 81) or a hymn based on a psalm. Write it with markings—for solos, small groups, *forte, pianissimo*—so it reflects your study of it and makes it easy for the readers to memorize it (much like the Hebrew poets used parallelism).

❏ Sing a psalm with one tune, then try it with another tune. How does the character of the psalm change? Or sing the same tune with two different texts. Use the metrical index in your hymnal to come up with other combinations. (Don't necessarily limit yourself to psalm texts. It's an interesting way to explore your hymnal!)

❏ Pray a psalm. Here is a method advocated by Presbyterian minister Gerrit S. Dawson: Begin by reading the psalm enough times to carry parts with you through the day. Then imagine situations in which these feelings could be evoked. Finally, wait, look, and listen for people who could be the focus for the intercession; you may know them or not. Dawson warns us to avoid the following traps, however: (1) Don't wallow in your emotions or those of the psalm. Intercede for others, not for self. (2) Don't spend lots of time wondering how the theology of the psalm fits with your overall theology. (3) Avoid a Messiah complex, believing that everything depends on the efficacy of your prayer. Empathy is not the same as God's grace.

❏ If they have not already been suggested, sing "Joyful, Joyful, We Adore Thee" (HWB 71, CH 2), "Awake, Arise, O Sing a New Song" (HWB 56), "With Happy Voices Singing" (HWB 83), or "Jubliate Deo"

(HWB 103), a Taizé song that can be sung as a round or dressed up with instrumental parts.

2. Sing to the Lord in the Company of the Faithful: Hymns of Praise

❑ Read Psalm 113. Write a cinquain on the theme of God's concern for the poor and needy. A cinquain is a five-line poem:

Line 1 - one word subject (such as "God")
Line 2 - two words which describe the subject in line one
Line 3 - three words about the subject
Line 4 - four words describing your feelings about the subject
Line 5 - one word synonym for the subject

❑ Find at least three hymns in your hymnal that praise God, but in different musical styles. Praise doesn't have to be repetitious or raucous. Is restrained praise still praise? Examples: "Praise the Lord" (HWB 52); "Who Is So Great a God" (HWB 62); "Asithi: Amen" (HWB 64); Father God, You Are Holy" (HWB 78); "Still, I Search for My God" (HWB 88).

❑ Read Psalm 96. Create a refrain and sing it between each verse or two of the psalm, as you read it aloud again. Examples:

- refrain of "For the Beauty of the Earth" (to the tune DIX): (CH 56, HWB 89)
- a refrain from a Taizé song: "Alleluia" (HWB 101) or "Gloria" (HWB 204, CH 34)
- "Awake, Arise" (HWB 56)
- Caribbean Hallelujah (CH 41)
- "Let the Heavens Be Glad" (HWB 187)
- portions of "Great Is the Lord" (HWB 87)

❑ Psalms 46, 96, and 113 are communal psalms, songs appropriate for experiences the whole community shares. Can you think of times when the whole community rallied together for praise, or for comfort? What has been a "big deal" for your community? Examples are natural disasters and responses to them, or the traumas of deaths of leaders: John F. Kennedy, Martin Luther King, Jr., Mother Teresa, Diana. If you were to help plan a community worship service for such a time, what hymns would you choose?

- ❑ As a group, work together to create a list of the attributes of God. Make it as long as you want; don't worry about repeating yourself; practice stream-of-consciousness praising; let ideas feed each other. Bookend it with acclamations of thanks. Do you have a psalm?

- ❑ Choose one or two hymns on the theme of community to sing together with your covenant group. There may be one or two that are especially meaningful for your group.

- ❑ If you have not already done so, sing the hymns listed under item 1 of Personal Preparation.

3. You Set the Earth on Its Foundation: Creation Hymns

- ❑ Go outside shoeless, if possible. Feel the earth on your feet, sit on the ground. In what part of your body do you most feel praise for creation? With God on your mind, what songs do you feel like singing? Try "Still, I Search for My God" (HWB 88).

- ❑ What *place* evokes prayer from you? Share a description of the spot you consider the most beautiful on earth. Can you choose just one?

- ❑ Talk to your plants. What would you tell them about their Creator?

- ❑ Bring something from your home that turns your mind to creation (potting soil, a vegetable you grew, a houseplant, water, insects, pets, a child).

- ❑ Think of the process you go through to invite someone for a meal in your home. Beginning with the invitation, take note of each thing you do to be a good host, to make the visit pleasant and/or special for your guest.

- ❑ Write a litany of Genesis 1:1–2:4a. Use the repeated phrases as the litany response.

- ❑ Choose one or two hymns on the theme of creation to sing together with your covenant group. If they haven't already been suggested, sing "Morning Has Broken" (HWB 648, CH 53); "This Is My Father's World" (CH 59, HWB 154); "I Sing the Mighty Power of God" (HWB 46); "Many and Great, O God" (HWB 35, CH 58); "Cantemos al Señor" (CH 60, HWB 55).

Suggestions for Sharing and Prayer 51

4. Restore Us Again!: Songs of Lament

❏ Compose a lament (or suggest one from a hymn or the Psalms) to send to someone you know who is suffering.

❏ Widen your scope. Send messages of hope to Amnesty International (try http://www.amnesty.org for more information). They forward personal notes to political prisoners around the world.

❏ Read as many different Bible translations as possible of Psalm 85:10-11, and do a comparison study of this beautiful picture of restoration. Create a litany of the different versions with your covenant group.

❏ First read each psalm for this session (13, 22, 85) as a psalm for personal use. Then read them again, this time as communal psalms. Do any of the three work better as personal rather than communal psalms (or vice versa)? Why? What's the difference?

❏ Have everyone read Psalm 22 through once silently. Then underline words and phrases that strike you for any reason—either because of the way they sound, because of the images they evoke, or because you connect with what the line says, or just because you like the word. Now have an expressive reader read the psalm aloud. The catch is that the reader won't be reading alone. Each person will join in reading their underlined words and phrases aloud whenever the reader comes to those words. Encourage people not to worry if they are not completely in unison. Simply say the underlined words aloud with as much expression and passion as they want when the reader gets there. This type of group reading adds a communal, interesting texture to the sound of the psalm.

❏ I've heard a story about a clown who, in a worship service, mimed a lament for a congregation that had lost a child. How would you choreograph the *end* of the lament—the expression of trust?

❏ Choose one or two hymns on the theme of sorrow/lament to sing together with your covenant group.

❏ If they haven't already been suggested, sing "Lord, Listen to Your Children Praying" (HWB 353, CH 305); a setting of "Dona Nobis Pacem" (HWB 346, CH 297); "My God, My God, Why" (HWB 248, an Anglican chant).

5. Songs of Thanksgiving

❑ Choose one or two hymns on the theme of thanksgiving to sing together with your covenant group.

❑ Try this exercise. It is not as easy as it may appear, yet it has the potential for dramatically changing relationships. Each time you meet or talk with a brother or sister from your church family, pray silently—"I give thanks to my God always for you" (1 Cor. 1:4). We may struggle sometimes to find something to be thankful for, but the prayer itself can lead to an attitude of thanks. What if you were aware that each time someone met you, they were praying this prayer?

❑ You've heard the phrase "Count your blessings." Do it! Make a list (or use the list you compiled during your Personal Preparation time) of what God has done for you personally, for your covenant group, for your family, and for your congregation. Put a time frame on it: yesterday, in the past week, in the past year. Be as specific as you can.

❑ Write a litany of what God has done in your lives and the life of your congregation. Choose a refrain which states or implies thanksgiving. It could be spoken, such as "God's steadfast love endures forever" or sung, such as "We thank thee all, our God, with hearts and hands and voices."

❑ Make a conscious effort to do one "random act of kindness" as an expression of thanks. Use the book itself, or brainstorm acts in your covenant group. How many can you come up with?

❑ If they haven't already been suggested, sing, "We Give Thanks unto You" (HWB 161), "Now Thank We All Our God" (HWB 85/86, CH 715/716).

6. Here Is My Servant, My Chosen: Servant Songs

❑ Choose one or two hymns on the theme of servanthood to sing together with your covenant group.

❑ If you can, get a copy of the *text only* of Handel's oratorio *The Messiah* (G. Schirmer's edition provides this). With your Bible in hand, mark Handel's text wherever you find actual text or allusion to portions of the Servant Songs from Isaiah 42:1-4; 49:1-6; 50:4-11; 52:13–53:12. It may not be easy, but try reading the Servant Songs as if

Suggestions for Sharing and Prayer 53

Jesus had not yet been born (which is, of course, when they were written). What is your experience reading this way?

❑ Search your hymnal for hymns that contain the text of or allusions to the Servant Songs from Isaiah. Try it first without checking the indexes in your hymnal, and see how many you can think of from memory. Then supplement your study with newspaper or news magazine consisting of the stories of servanthood you've collected in Personal Preparation. Include stories of servants who suffer and stories where service is rewarded. How does such a paper change your ideas of the weekly news?

❑ Discover where these images of "man of sorrows" and "suffering servant" have been used in religious art and music (other than hymnody); bring in art pieces that depict these images.

❑ If they haven't already been suggested, sing "Man of Sorrows, What a Name" (HWB 258), "O Sacred Head, Now Wounded" (HWB 252, CH 202), "Jesu, Jesu, Fill Us with Your Love" (CH 600), and the three contemporary hymns listed at the end of the Understanding section.

7. My Soul Magnifies the Lord: Nativity Songs

❑ Choose one or two hymns on the theme of advent/Christmas to sing together with your covenant group.

❑ Light one candle as someone reads the text of Mary's Magnificat (Luke 1:46-55). Then sing together a musical setting of it. What is the most comforting thing about the song? What makes you squirm? Why? (In this and the two readings that follow, have electric lights up only bright enough for seeing hymnals.)

❑ Light one candle as someone reads the text of Zechariah's Benedictus (Luke 1:67-79). Then sing together a musical setting of it. What is the most comforting thing about the song? What makes you squirm? Why?

❑ Light one candle as someone reads the text of Simeon's Nunc Dimittis (Luke 2:29-32). Then sing together a musical setting of it. What is the most comforting thing about the song? What makes you squirm? Why?

- ❏ Compare the Song of Hannah (1 Sam. 2:1-10) and the Magnificat (Luke 1:46-55).

- ❏ If they haven't already been suggested, sing "My Soul Proclaims with Wonder" (HWB 181) and the Taizé renditions of the Nunc Dimittis or Magnificat.

8. The Greatest of These: Hymns of Love

- ❏ The celebrated author C. S. Lewis wrote a lot about love before he really fell in love. He'd probably concur with Paul that it's a lot easier to talk about love than it is to do it. Read his *A Grief Observed* (take notes), or watch the movie *Shadowlands*, based on the story of his marriage. Discuss the book and movie in your covenant group.

- ❏ Choose one or two hymns on the theme of *agape* love to sing together with your covenant group. See how many different musical styles of "love" songs are brought to your group.

- ❏ What is the most profound expression of love you've seen in the past month? Ponder this question in silence before answering.

- ❏ Conduct a symbolic service of *agape* love with one of the following: feetwashing, hand or neck massage, handwashing. Are there other "services" that could symbolize this love, something that is at once intimate, hospitable, and necessary?

- ❏ If they haven't already been suggested, sing "Heart with Loving Heart United" (HWB 420) and "Bless'd Be the Tie that Binds" (HWB 421, CH 433).

9. The Image of the Invisible God: Hymns of Faith

- ❏ Choose one or two hymns that you can embrace as statements of your faith. Sing them together with your covenant group.

- ❏ Read Colossians 1:15-20 and Philippians 2:5-11. In your Bible, or on a copy of these hymns, underline all parts that you can affirm in your own faith. Are there any that you cannot affirm? Talk it over with your covenant group.

- ❏ Critique written affirmations of faith found in your hymnal. Do any of these put you at cross-purposes with other demands for your allegiance, such as the Pledge of Allegiance, for example?

- ❏ Anyone being licensed or ordained for ministry has to write a faith statement, and many faith traditions require baptismal candidates to do it. If you were being baptized next week, what statement of faith would you make before your faith community? Make it a song, if you like.

- ❏ Paraphrase the Christ hymns (Col. 1:15-20; Phil. 2:5-11) in words for today.

- ❏ If it has not already been suggested, sing "Creator of the Stars of Night" (HWB 177, CH 127, a plainsong chant with allusions to Col. 1:15-20) and "Christ Is Risen! Shout Hosanna!" (HWB 272; CH 222).

10. Worthy Is the Lamb: Hymns in Revelation

- ❏ Choose one or two hymns that you would want to send to people who are being persecuted. You can do this without personally knowing people in this position, but it helps if you have someone in mind. You could even choose people from other centuries, such as martyrs for the faith. Sing them together with your covenant group.

- ❏ With your covenant group, chant the following powerful Revelation hymns antiphonally: Revelation 5:9-14 and Revelation 19:5, 6b-8.

- ❏ Play hymn charades. Choose about ten well-known hymns, and put titles in a container (slips of paper with first lines only). Divide into two teams, and play the game. Afterward draw comparisons about the way you used picture language in the game and the way the book of Revelation uses picture language to send its message of hope in a world gone wrong.

- ❏ Gather information about Christians being persecuted today. Sometimes there are Internet sites that post updates. Be in prayer for individual Christians you know of who are in danger of dying for their faith, or who are struggling financially because they have made unpopular faith choices. As an alternative, use a book of martyrs' prayers for your intercessory prayer time (Duane W. H. Arnold has a nice anthology called *Prayers of the Martyrs*, Zondervan Publishing House, 1991).

- ❏ If possible, make plans to visit a cathedral together, preferably for a worship time or a concert. What is it that makes music seem transcendent in such places?

❏ John left a verbal time capsule filled with symbols of his time; his message was "Hold on, God's love wins out in the end." Make your own time capsules for the millennium. Put in copies of symbols and hymns that express how you see God active in your congregation. What would you like people of the future to know about the hymns that really speak to you?

Other Covenant Bible Studies

1 Corinthians: The Community Struggles (Inhauser) $5.95
Abundant Living: Wellness from a Biblical Perspective
  (Rosenberger) $4.95
Biblical Imagery for God (Bucher) $5.95
Covenant People (Heckman/Gibble) $5.95
Daniel (Ramirez) $5.95
Ephesians: Reconciled in Christ (Ritchey Martin) $5.95
Esther (Roop) $5.95
The Gospel of Mark (Ramirez) $5.95
In the Beginning (Kuroiwa) $5.95
James: Faith in Action (Young) $5.95
Jonah: God's Global Reach (Bowser) $4.95
The Life of David (Fourman) $4.95
The Lord's Prayer (Rosenberger) $4.95
Love and Justice (O'Diam) $4.95
Many Cultures, One in Christ (Garber) $5.95
Mystery and Glory in John's Gospel (Fry) $5.95
Paul's Prison Letters (Bynum) $5.95
Presence and Power (Dell) $4.95
The Prophecy of Amos and Hosea (Bucher) $5.95
Psalms (Bowman) $4.95
Real Families: From Patriarchs to Prime Time (Dubble) $5.95
Revelation: Hope for the World in Troubled Times (Lowery) $5.95
Sermon on the Mount (Bowman) $4.95
A Spirituality of Compassion: Studies in Luke (Finney/Martin) .. $5.95
When God Calls (Jessup) $5.95
Wisdom (Bowman) $5.95

To place an order, call Brethren Press toll-free Monday through Friday, 8 A.M. to 4 P.M., at **800-441-3712**, or fax an order to **800-667-8188** twenty-four hours a day. Shipping and handling will be added to each order. For a full description of each title, ask for a free catalog of these and other Brethren Press titles.

Visa and MasterCard accepted. Prices subject to change.

Brethren Press® • *faithQuest*® • 1451 Dundee Ave., Elgin, IL 60120-1694
800-441-3712 (orders) • 800-667-8188

MANCHESTER COLLEGE LIBRARY

3 9315 01033917 1

220.07 P249h c.2
Parrott, Mary Anne, 1943-
Hymns and songs of the Bible

DATE DUE

DATE DUE

WITHDRAWN
from
Funderbur